"... (A) delightful and disturbing read. A flurry of allusions, of histories, of personal disasters, all of it lightened with insight and a sly, sexy humor."
—**Arthur Smith, author of** *The Fortunate Era*

In *The Branches, the Axe, the Missing*, Charlotte Pence goes beyond situating the personal within the contexts of science and history; she instead finely mortises the evolution of the human form with that of her own poetic form. This carefully shaped sequence reminds us that the "sizzle-spit of fat striking flame" remains part cause, part sustenance--and is indivisible, finally, from "that first word, that first word / that spiked a whole new species."
—**Claudia Emerson, author of the Pulitzer Prize-winning collection** *Late Wife* **and** *Figure Studies*

Many Small Fires

poems by Charlotte Pence

*I have such fond
memories of my
time here. Thank
you for being
so supportive of my
poetry.*

*Charlotte
2015
Belmont*

Black
Lawrence
Press

www.blacklawrence.com

Executive Editor: Diane Goettel
Cover and Book Design: Amy Freels

Copyright © 2015 Charlotte Pence
ISBN: 978-1-62557-918-8

Published 2015 by Black Lawrence Press.
Printed in the United States.

To Adam, my husband, my home, my fire,
who said: Write what you're interested in—
and what you fear.

CONTENTS

AUTHOR'S NOTE

When I say that this book is ecological, I am not referring to the widely used secondary definition, which aligns social action with environmental protection. I mean the book is ecological in its primary sense: the branch of biology that considers the relationship of organisms to one another and to their physical surroundings. In many ways, all good poetry does just that; it hones in on our physical and emotional connections and acknowledges nature's role in our lives—be it destructive, rejuvenative, or exculpatory. The poem is its own world in which each line break, each detail, each letter depends on what comes before and after, in the same way a bone needs another bone to become a body. The poem's only incompleteness is its need for a reader.

Many Small Fires attempts to make explicit several connections we, as a species, seem to intuit. The second section, previously published as a chapbook and written as one long poem in which facing pages reply to each other, brings in recent theories of evolutionary anthropology to shed light on the complex human invention that is community. Community is not only as necessary to the human race as fire, but also potentially as deadly. While we need one another, we don't always know how to support one another. Even when we try, we sometimes fail. No parent, I imagine, ever plans to disappoint. No child does either. Yet how often are those stories told? The book's second section brings in facts regarding our evolution from an upright but ape-like species to what we are now: fast-fingered lovers of light (fire, electricity, computer chips, cell phones), community (virtual, real, connected by memories, motives, and DNA) and motion (planes, cars, bikes, anything that allows us to leave and return).

This sense of interconnectivity permeates throughout the book. My husband and I were backpacking through Indonesia when I began writing about my father, who has been homeless since I was eighteen because of his paranoid schizophrenia. It was a three-month trip that we repeated the following summer. During these two years, I studied the intersections between the evolution of human physiology and human behavior such as pair-bonding and settlement creation. I wondered about whatever enabled our species to form a home in the first place. Luckily for me, much has been written on the subject, albeit outside the realm of the Humanities. Also luckily for me, I happened to be in a place where some of the most exciting discoveries were being made about our species. Indonesia, specifically the remote island of Flores where I visited, is home to the most recent, confirmed discovery of a distinct species named Homo floresiensis. More commonly known as the "hobbit people" because of their short stature, this species suggests many exciting things about evolutionary rates. What is indisputable, however, is that this species lived at the same time as modern man. We thought we were alone, but we were not. As I began to reflect on my childhood, I did so amidst the backdrop of Indonesia, finding not only a thematic resonance but also an emotional one. As all travelers know, never is a sense of home as clear as when we feel the lack of it.

Considering the amount of science in this book, the notes at the end might prove useful. Also, I would recommend reading the book in sequence rather than in sips.

Finally, if one feels so inclined to help the homeless after reading this book, I would suggest engagement with organizations that follow the Housing First approach. As opposed to the traditional housing readiness tactic that requires evidence of stability before a home is provided, Housing First immediately provides permanent housing, along with supportive services. Not only has it proven effective, reducing homelessness in some cities by 50%, but it also has proven to save communities more money than the housing readiness approach because ERs, prisons, and detoxification centers are used less. Ultimately, the success of Housing First undercuts some firm-fisted American beliefs concerning self-sufficiency and autonomy. Housing First reminds us that we are still guided by fundamental needs such as shelter and that we are still one community, albeit fragmented. We are never able to free ourselves of each other, no matter how we might try. Let us celebrate our ancestral roots, and then turn toward the work of living together on this planet composed of many small fires.

... All must fall to the ground according to definite laws; but how simple is this problem compared to ... action and reaction ...

—From *On the Origin of Species* by Charles Darwin

ARGUMENT (1)

Wind bending a grove
Of bamboo. Thin-trunked.
Sound of an opening door.
I think of my father.

How through him—
    His Oreo-fat,
    His hardening cock,
    His long, curled lashes

I stutter-stepped into myself.
A woman
    In wonder.

Why do you write that stuff? my father interrupts.

What do you mean? About your cock?

No. That right there, he says, lifting his arms, glass of O.J. in one
hand, Little Debbie oatmeal cream pie in the other. He stands like
a Lady of the Scales statue—chewing a wad of snack cake.

What are you talking about? What's in my poems? How I see the world?

All of this, he says and circles his drink in the air. *This house. Our
family. You and me. You think it's everything.* He nods toward the
window. *But what's out there doesn't even begin it.*

I answer: *Yesterday I saw something I've never seen before: A canary-yellow web that only one spider in the world can weave. What do you think about that?*

He shrugs. *Charlotte, that's yesterday.*

I.

But the struggle almost invariably will be most severe between the individuals of the same species, for they frequent the same districts, require the same food, and are exposed to the same dangers.

—From *On the Origin of Species* by Charles Darwin

ARCHITECTURE OF THE VEIL

Islamic architecture often adorns the interior spaces as opposed to
the exterior spaces. Commonly known as the architecture of the
veil, this style alludes to the nature of the infinite.

Leaning over the low wall around our hotel roof, we are fooled
into thinking Jakarta below might be understood by echo,

by prayer calls, car horns, hot spoons scraping woks of *nasi goreng.*
Or by gazing down on *pishtaqs*, minarets, cannons fashioned

into fountains. All afternoon, the faithful go on being faithful.
The faithless, faithless. Each chasing piety with sugar and sticks.

Green-flanked smog shifts directions, sweeps the clouds
into crumbs, into evening, into this thing called the infinite.

The architecture here secludes its beauty to inner spaces,
to what cannot be seen from the street where a costumed

macaque flees under a soup stall, his frustration blooming
into soapsuds rushing the gutter. A walker passes by adding

a spoonful of blood to her thickening placenta; a beggar
irritates his toothache into stone. And the mosaics repeat

and spin their cobalt patterns until the moon quivers one day
forward—and no one notices except that two mangoes rot

while green on the tree. All the while, the prophets' daughters
strut by in their highest heels, poking the sun back

into the pieces it really is. This brokenness, we suspect,
is true about our own selves, despite the fluid strides we make

from city block to city block. We walk among sweet sulfur,
wondering what we cannot see, wondering which feast or fast

is behind which house's wall. In each of us, a stray dog forgets
to ask for home; a pack of roving hounds guards the door.

PIG AND A BOTTLE

—Funeral sacrifice in Sulawesi, Indonesia. June 2010.

The blood, too fresh for flies, a newly skinned
skull left to dry, but otherwise this dulled
dirt-patch where animals are sacrificed
is just another piece of empty ground.

I'm ten thousand miles from where I grew up
by S.D. Johnson Elementary.
At recess, we would search for a kidnapped girl,
also named Charlotte. We each hoped to get

lucky and be the one to find her skull.
See, Dad would say, *We're all the same. Don't act
so goody-goody. Who doesn't wanna see
the fat behind skin? Watch a person die?*

In front of me, the coffin shimmers under
the spread of red silk hand-stitched with one-inch
mirrors. If I approached, I'd see pieces
of myself. So, I watch a boy and his wiggly

muscles struggling to lift a pig who's strapped
to bamboo—its grill and grave. It thrashes out
of its rope, which sends the men scrambling away.
And right when I cheer this pig's escape, a warmth

wets my leg as a machete opens a buffalo's throat,
its blood spraying like water from a sprinkler.

Dad loved to tell me what he could do with
a beer bottle's broken neck. Take the glassed

peaks to the throat:
                   It gives like a pillow.
I'm not a pillow, I'd say.
                   Not today.
Tell me whose neck you took the bottle to?
                   Homeless guy. By the river after I bought him
                   the beer. And what you need to remember, Miss
                   Goody Goody: No one ever noticed.

AG RESEARCH©

We didn't understand what we were holding,
but knew both penis and vagina on the piglet
meant something. We answered its squeals
with clucks and shush. Took note of its moonish,
hard belly. Sang "Twinkle, Twinkle" to distract
from the ear tag's needle and punch. My body
was not the body the piglet longed for:
no mother's teat, swollen and flabby, spritzing
milk; no fur slicked with manured hay to wallow
and warm. But song is song. Sailors, chain gangs,
boys with Corvettes and girls with Hondas—
we need song. I broke a flute once to get inside
the soft pads of each key. Found only metal and holes
and cold. That's the way with searching, isn't it?
We think we know before we know. In this world,
even babies hear their names before they're born.

BARDO (1)

My childhood chore was to shoo away two ghosts Dad didn't like: Grimekle and Had. Had stole oil from our Oldsmobile, streaked his cheeks with it until the car burned dry and caught fire. Grimekle tramped through the garden after hard rains, making the dirt rocky, useless. He would machete down Dad's cornstalks soon as they reached four feet tall, forcing Dad to stop writing his letters to ex-bosses, come outside with pencil paused over clipboard, yell about my neglect—everything hulking around mid-sentence.

Like us, they worried what was real. What passed for normal. Each night on the way to bed, they paused with Dad and me around our Van Gogh print. *Haystacks Under a Rainy Sky*. And each night Dad told us how Van Gogh cut off his ear and mailed it to a woman who scorned him. He would always say, "There's a man who knew how to show a bitch what she was missing."

Sometimes, I didn't notice the ghosts when they squatted motionless as pennies on our counter top. Sometimes I'd whisper how Dad was crazy. A pervert. They'd shrug as if to say, "That's life" or "Sorry." Once I suggested Van Gogh painted with his cut-off ear, his paint strokes the size of an ear lobe. They laughed, called me a dumb kid, teased me for believing in spooky stories.

They passed their plans from one world to the next through the spilt salt grains at the dinner table, as if salt itself were the message, as if we had long agreed to this life of passing notes between the in-between.

MY FATHER'S NIPPLES

I.
Fat, pastry-dough sacks, tipped
with cone-shaped nipples. Or maybe,
tips of lemons. No—more like
bloated pieces of candy corn,
raging colors of that autumn,
and the maple we sat under as he
revealed his plans for other girls. And me.

II.
A father and daughter under a tree—
                so tall it scratched all day at the sun.
Branches gnarled but striving up and away,
something Frost might say a boy could climb
                to leave earth
                a little while.

III.
From a distance,
perhaps the kitchen window over the sink,
his hand cupping mine might have seemed loving.

Index finger circling, circling inside the palm—
        This is how you masturbate.
        This is how you kiss a man's nipple.

IV.
One side of his chest reminded me of:
    a beached jellyfish,
    a strong hope,
    a deflating ball

that sat all winter in a hole outside our door.
Twenty feet down, a maple root must have broken
part of the earth, pulling down part of the drive,
flattening one side of the ball, so even the earth
leaves itself for a little while.

V.
I cannot leave this earth, but I can cross
a splayed log that fell across the creek once spring
began its thaw; I can stare at the shifting light

through the shivering branches; and I can decide
to love what isn't attached to what I hate.

Separate the log,
the crossing,
the leaves,
the brother watching
at the kitchen window
from the maple,
the trunk,
the body,
the weight of the body.

Even relinquish my hate of this earth forbidding
me to climb away, giving only an afternoon
by the creek under the damp-green rhododendrons
where humidity and ghost-thin mosquitoes hover
alongside something else best not to name.

NORMALIZATION OF DEVIANCE

1986, winter of Challenger disaster, O-rings,
solid rocket boosters, southern cold snaps.
Dad blinked at a break in the news coverage,
walked out the door, leaving my brother and me
saying for days, *He was right here*—
as if the man were a ring of lost keys.

He returned six weeks later, but this scene
repeated into routine. His duffel bag remained
on the hearth, half-filled with Twinkies,
yardage stats on touchdown passes,
newspaper clippings on the sheriff's
helicopter purchases. Always unknown

when he would come and go. My brother and I
were sixteen and ten. Ran the house accordingly.
I'd spit in the stew, forgetting I'd have to eat it, too.
My brother paid me a quarter a day not to cry.
Dad downplayed the returns to a simple *Hey*,
head nod, stacks of 100s for groceries and heat.

Five years earlier we'd day-tripped to the future:
viewed Space Shuttle Columbia, OV-102 being built.
It loomed over Florida's flatness, sat stiff
and upright like a scared school girl. The metal
scaffolding alongside it, an organized mess
of angles, impressive as the shuttle itself.

I tripped on the newly paved tarmac, still ridged
from no wear. Dad began yelling how he'd sue,
told me it would be the ugliest scar, doom me
to short men who played guitar. His parenting style
was listing off dramatic dangers: poltergeist head-
swivels, lawn-mowered toes, detached retinas.

But my fears were the seemingly harmless: a father
in a white bath robe standing by my bed, a black
government Buick pulling into the drive. So, I wasn't
surprised when the billion-dollar marvel turned to dust
over the Texas sky. A bundle of titanium brought down
by a single cut from a small piece of falling foam.

MY FATHER SPEAKS OF THIEVES

My house shall be called the house of prayer;
but ye have made it a den of thieves.
—Matthew 21:13

Let's imagine a world of lack. Lack of luck, steady
money. The way the road shortens closer to home.

Let's imagine a girl of extras. Freckles, glares, stories,
and friends. A girl who sells rotten tomatoes
at the market for more money than the good ones.

Let's imagine the world as it is. Of course people
were selling pigeons in the Temple, that den
of thieves, house of dens. Need is not thievery.

Let's imagine a man asking his eight-year-old for a loan.
She draws up a contract on her toybox. Her stuffed
animals lined up like prisoners before a firing squad,
everyone watching as she says: *With interest.*

CAST-OFFS

What we remember gains value from what we forget.
Where is the autumn in Persephone's myth? The yellow
lost to the bleach? The second pair of baby shoes?

Such need to feel significant in a world that confirms
insignificance. The search for bones and bowls,
bits of bomb shells, even though museums are full of them.

What we know gains clarity from what we misunderstand.
The bristled, wagging tail of a revving-up dog. A "sure"
that means no. Brightness of ice on a black country road.

THE DIAGNOSIS: PARANOID SCHIZOPHRENIA

When the doctor scrims back your bed curtain,
    again, you see she's just another accomplice
        in a white lab coat, another archetype of hope.

And the fake flower tucked in her hair tries to say,
    I'm different. I'm happy. I'm here—for you.
        This time she delivers a name for the same thing

they've been treating you for all your life: *schizo,*
    split and divide, from the Greek, "of shattered mind…"
        or something like that, and you, still strapped

with canvas wraps, test the right ankle, the left, the wrists,
    ask: *Could you bring me that axe?* Always a do-er,
        a chop-chop-chopper, you can hear that helicopter

coming back and a cough that colludes out in the hall,
    another shill scribbling on the scrips pad, one more
        cure-all toward the goal of "functioning adult."

You know the intricacies of Haldol, Trilafon,
    Prolizin. Know the younger models:
        positive-Sally-sounding Abilify, the sexy Saphris,

and her fat twin Thiothixene. Know, too, that nothing
    will work for twenty percent of people like you,
        "treatment resistant" one therapist admitted.

So, you are demanding now, *Just bring me that axe*,
maybe even yelling. And they are hovering,
all of them hovering: the flower and the hall,

the coats and the carts, the machine
outside the window and the gun-round-growl
of its blades that will not, will not stop.

MEMORY CORRUPTION: CINDERELLA ALWAYS

the kitchen's chimney

was overtaken

the family could

only boil

one daughter later swore

ants never existed

she built terrariums

inside the house's steps

the daughter kept

a duster

it smelled like sweat

between a man's

a sister told her

you'll marry

she nodded but

knew they would

she also knew he *was*

a fine gentleman

another sister

challenged her

Cinderella took

the banister

closed her eyes so

she couldn't

of course

she kept her eyes

the blurring living

room unsettled

KNEW SHE'D LOSE A SHOE

by knitted ant trails

not smoke their meat

only mortar crumbs

with hinges and sally-ports

to wipe each cactus

thighs

a fine gentleman

divorce

just dull

said *race you*

down for the speed

see the fall

wide open

her balance

ants in the chimney

there were points awarded

ink was already

so she chose the

or had she not

like every woman

she wanted to pretend

there were

she smelled of smoke

what was missing

and the house being a one-

twitched their antennae

maybe three

wet

orange

lost her

who divorces

the marriage

however

and danced all the 80s

were the terrariums

story rancher had neither

into touchdown signs

stitches and a cast

on the marriage license

leg cast

shoe yet?

clarity came afterward

never happened

certain proofs

nights in town

of cacti

a banister nor stairs

DIVINING

i.

We are a train, father and daughter, car and caboose, divining rods in front of chests. We are water-witching, doodlebugging. Divining.

We are marching. I tell him we are ready to parade down Main Street. And I'll write our banner slogan: *Call Spike. He'll treat you right.* He says, *Shush. You have to feel it. Shush.*

So, I wait for the twitch, wait for the sticks to cross. To x. Follow his pace, head down, feet placed in eight-inch patterns. Listen to whatever it is that rides the wind. Butterfly. Apple. Old bell. Nothing. I am learning how to listen to nothing. More real than what is there. I hear his back sweating, the sticks not moving, the promise from earlier in the morning: *We'll get rich. You would like that, huh? Be like your friends.*

His stick rigs. Or doesn't. We stand so still I see how much everything moves in this yard: the leaves, the squirrels, the shrubs. We stand so still Dad says, *I can feel the ground soften. Water. There is water.*

Or maybe not. I realize we do not have a machine to drill a well— nor do we know what prevents a well from caving in. I can hear his face reddening, and so I tell him I don't want a well. I want what I have: a father who is a diviner.

ii.

Tell me a secret, I asked him later. *Tell me how you know where there is water.*

He said: *It's like you can fall down. And just drop and drop and drop. It's like a grave that never ends. No one or no thing there with you.*

Like when the girl fell in the old well last summer and died? When all the news crews came out and camped by the hole?

No, not like that at all. She was one of the lucky ones. People didn't forget her. Promise me, Charlotte: You'll never put me in a hole. You'll never bury me and walk away.

"IT WOULD BE NICE TO HAVE A WHOLE COMPLETE MALE"

> —Quote from archeologist Mike Morwood in
> "Hobbit Skeleton Changes Evolution"

☐

Down in that 130-foot cave
where archeologists search
for whole complete men,
what do they see
inside the small skulls
they hold in their hands?
    Teeth shorn from tearing hides,
    cracked jaws healed by time.

Or simply old paths?
    Brain curls
    and switchbacks
    scientists can name:
    Brodmann's Area 10,
    Broca and Wernicke's regions.

What don't they see?
    Memories of shivering nights
    feeding the moon orange,
    raw water lilies bent toward mystery,
    cut heels from a rat's long lather.

So they dig and dig
    this island inside out

while rats around them
grow to the size of dogs.

And the whole complete male they search for,
        two meters tall instead of three,
        brain a third the size,

is not the man beside them
        who steals a pinch of dirt
        and sucks it like cane.

He is not who they look for,
        being more than bone,
        being more than clay
        being more than iron
        and fatigue.

□

After seven days at sea, land beneath my feet
heaves and sinks like a sleeping man's belly.
I'm finally here on the island of Flores
where archeologists raise their spikes, chink

deep into the earth while I, a woman in a white dress,
walk the little square. *The streets,* the townspeople
chatter, *are so ugly. Please forgive. Please understand.* We speak
non-stop, which means it's summer and palms rub

with blisters and chilé. A short man with six ears
of corn under one arm, tin under the other, tells me
people call him a hobbit. *But I am tall*, he insists,
Tall as any tree I need to climb. He asks if I want a tour

of stories: nine children, two wives, one foot taken
by thieves. He asks if I am here to write about them,
and I almost tell the truth. Instead, I say yes,
I'll write of the men in those caves being cleaned

with pastry brushes that wipe bone from bone.
Men who, we are told, don't measure out as men.
Where have we heard this story before? *Please forgive*,
he interrupts, *the streets are littered with what we have used.*

SIGNS AND SYMPTOMS [MAY] INCLUDE DELUSIONS

Pitch pines,
     sap suckers,
turkey oaks,
     tit mice,
surround, surround
     this man working,
leaning left
     on his ladder, right
foot a toe-
     tip-touch
as he goes to roof
     his girl's playhouse.
This man knows
     to number, to name,
accounting a means
     of first strike.
So … sweet birch,
     borer bees,
sedge wren,
     robins, robins,
whorish robins,
     willing to roost
on his shoulder
     should he let them.
He swears he feels
     a hard stare

as he screws down
        the starter strip
on this simple grey
        gable roof,
no valleys,
        no hips,
just one pair
        of pitch planes.
He works right
        and uphill for hours
until it's time
        to tar shingles
to buckling flange.
        He fears the black
ooze glue
        that grabs fast
as handcuffs,
        that could hold-drown
a saber-tooth
        in a tar pit.
Cicadas sing,
        twining their timbres
so loud
        some thoughts
can't think,
        so he climbs
to the ridge top
        and straddles tall.
Fists clench,
        then unclench,

decision made,
        decided against.
And then, she's there.
        Through the cedar
limbs he glimpses
        the girl glaring,
sitting cross-
        legged, leaning
over her notebook,
        always note-
note-noting
        and staring straight
at him, at his
        eyes as if she
sees nothing,
        sees no one.

"LIFE IS LONG AND FULL OF ACTION AND COLOR"

—Charles Darwin

The Indonesian mountain weasel   pulls
herself up to the next
branch,   her tail   a fifth limb.
     The higher   she climbs
     the thinner the bark,
unlike   the scabby trunk   where wood
     … soft as berries.
A nest of fledging mynahs   close enough
she can see   one   glinty,   stand-alone
piece of hatchling fuzz.
          A thing so new to this earth it lacks
all color.   She strikes
     with her fat-rippled body,   and the bird,
if it opened its eyes,   would have seen
          the thousand colors of   life.

II.

It is not a question of whether we as a whole will be "saved" or "lost," but of how much of us.

—From *The Gospel According to Darwin*
by Woods Hutchinson (1898)

THE BRANCHES, THE AXE, THE MISSING

☐

What small mammals

did we roast in the fire?

What first story did we

tell? Something about

longing. About loss:

The big one.

The got-away.

□

At the turn into the driveway, her headlights reveal something
  dark.

Light shining on darkness.

A limb has fallen, twenty-foot long and branded with many
  branches.

It is thirty-four degrees.

Drizzling.

She wants to be warm, eat that leftover lasagna, drink a single
  glass of boxed red wine.

The engine idles.

She has just returned from her last act as a married woman:
  mailing the new-ex his car title. He wanted a copy faxed and
  the original over-nighted.

She can hear now the car part that scrapes under the hood.

She buttons her coat, lifts the collar, gets out.

Grabs the branch by the base.

Her hands slide down wet slime of turkey-tail mushrooms in
  bloom.

She pauses.

Begins again.

It takes five tugs, a deep drag. Moon seeps through to a shine.

How long has it been since she has done something as
fundamental as this?

Cleared a path, been wet, been cold.

She decides not to wipe off her hands.

Scent of wet dog shit limps over from the neighbor's yard. Their
windows are ice-black.

Something about this feeling is honest. Like nakedness.

Like this November moon, color of silk, neither white nor silver.

Something she wants to conquer and can't.

□

We were born from wood and fire.
Roasting small mammals as we sat
in circles. The sizzle-spit of fat striking

flame. And outside the circle: darkness.
Stalk of hyena. Crick-shift of his step.
Then man lifting a torch—jab-jab-jabbing

that dark until the sounds flee back to the
quiet: sizzle-spits. Shifts of logs carboned
and bone-thin. Ashed by morning.

□

Biological anthropologists are discovering that
"we were born from wood
                              and fire" is less
figurative than it seemed.

Taming fire

                              led to
cooking   which led to
more calories   which led to
bigger brains   to
language   speech   communities
w/ clusters of moms, dads, Bobbies & Sallies.

But w/ everything gained, there is loss. What
                    is the equation for this?
Simply: 1+1 is no longer one?
                              With taming
fire   what was lost?

□

The wet, the cold,
makes her think of Spike,
her father. Or perhaps
what makes her think
of her father
is the house itself,
heater clicking on
as she opens the door,
stargazers' scent
drifting from the hall,
red-packaged log
on the hearth, and
the dog by this log,
whining because
it has not seen her
in five hours. She
has not seen her
father in fifteen years.
He is homeless,
a fact many friends
don't even know. If
she is asked why
her father moved
her family as often as
every six months, she
replies that he has
a "mercurial disposition."
Mercurial an SAT word.

She does not know
how to spell
schizophrenic.
Pedophilia she learned
in third grade.

□

Georgia July and the thought of ice storms occurred to her
father.

Fifty-three loblolly pines surrounded their house back then.
Fifty-three pines that could ice-over, splinter, crash the roof.

They sat on their porch next to the strawberry patch that had
given up only three berries all season.

She rarely weeded. She was ten.

Her dad liked quoting Frost and his proclamations of the world's
end—*...in fire, some say ice.*

He kept ten full gallons of gasoline in the garage.

One chainsaw.

Cut to fall away from the house, those pines went down in seven
hours.

A boy biked by with his sister on the handlebars. She wore a
headband with bunny ears. Silver fabric where pink should
have been.

The sound of falling pines was new to her, yet recognizable.

A sound slow to finish like stacked plates falling after an earthquake. Something impossible to stop, forcing one to stand by and watch.

Just before dark, the chainsaw quieted and the bike squeaked by. The boy wore the ears now. There was no sister.

She began walking through each fallen tree top.

Such rooms within those limbs. Sometimes she did pull-ups to the next firred space. Other times, she ape-swung and jumped down.

In one nest's weave, she found foil from a chip bag and a wobbly line of red string. Two weeks ago, she had torn her red dress at the edge of these woods.

Aren't you one lucky kid? her father called from somewhere.

She stopped moving, let the tree hide her. And it did, towering even as it lay on its side.

□

Upright   but apelike Australopithecines?
                    Knife-making habilines?
Maybe Homo erectus himself
                    who, if given a suit,
could walk the streets   like any
                    overlooked male?

Maybe the first species   to strike fire

did so by all lucky-dumb.

                    Some brute banging blind
pyrites against flint   in hopes
of an axe.

            Or maybe some girl   tripped,
        her deerskin shawl
                                        dipping
            into a gas-fired strip   in Antalya.

Or maybe our instinct to taunt led to fire:
cocky   juveniles
                    jousting each other
with smoldering twigs
        after lightning   struck the savannah.

□

However the story began,   we know
   its middles,   know
how taming fire kicked us
out of arrested development.

          We know
we've experienced
four major spikes in our evolution:

Adding roots to the diet of foliage=the 1st
Adding meat   =the 2nd
Adding cooking   =the 3rd

And language bottle-rocketed us into the
                4th.

Fire and evolution converging:
    breaking box-locked mussels,
    splitting   barley seeds,
    sterilizing   water's secrets.
Ekua tubers, cattails, water lily roots
all simmering in tortoise shells
and served family-style
around the fire where someone eventually
   thought   to ask: how was your day?

And what we ate, changed our bodies:
    smaller teeth,   thinner

jaws,   shorter guts.
  Cooking doing the work   our bodies
once did.
              With this newly discovered
time   and energy,
    the body reorganized.

Gave less to the gut and more to the brain,

greedy for glucose.   The brain
gulped it all,   gulped
more space,   more thought,
more this thing called self-aware,
    and now, so self-aware   we've located
and labeled it   Brodmann's Area 10.

□

Feeding oneself one fruit, one nut, one leaf
as monkeys feed ended with control of fire.
                                        We became
communal,
          Became communities of who does what—
          Who scoops honey from hives
          Who cuts tongue from antelope
          Who scrapes corn from husk.

                              We became
arranged
          Into cooks and hunters,
          Husbands and wives,
          Into worlds of many small fires and many small roofs.
          Fathers and daughters, lovers and ex-es,
connected
by a desire   to forget our histories.

□

Like kicking a pebble over a cliff and never

hearing it fall. Soon, you walk away

and forget about it.

Most of the time. Tonight, she is thinking about

two men, her father, now homeless, and her ex-husband.

She had been direct with both of them.

She reminded her ex that she had never

been in love. She told her father

he would drag her down with him.

She was right. They agreed. They are gone.

Like kicking a pebble over a cliff and never

hearing it fall. Soon, you walk away.

□

She does not know how
all this relates to when
sex was sex
or love was sex.

She does not know
the knowledge lost
before the mind
conceived of language,
conceived of sound
to represent
men   cup   couple of men.

The moment after we spoke
how did the world change?

[A warbled line—a branch—a feeling
of one limb leading to another.]

We look at this as progress.
Language as advancement.

In her small life, she
is happier than before.

Those two men
she didn't like are gone.
They were once with her
and now
they are not.   Blip of thought.
Flick of branch.

□

What was the mind like before language?

Needs.
> [A bird.]

Images.
> [Arc of bird's chest as it rises from a bay bush.]

Metaphor.
> [A man is the thrust of the bird's breast as it rises from a
> bay bush.]

Act.
> [A spreading of the bird's wings.
> A lifting.
> A spreading of the man's arms.
> A stilling.
> His feet still on the ground.]

□

This is all impossible. The description and the act of man imagining
to fly.

That story of Icarus
not flying, but falling:

A crack.
One crack to one crack to one crack until
a break.
A branch coming down.

This is the story we keep telling.

How the small world falls.

□

The groan of a car engine long ignored.

She hoped he heard what she was not saying.

They smelled of each other. Of the dog in the back seat. Of their friend's dog that they were just now leaving.

The yellow was seeping away from the morning sun, but humans have never feared the change to white-noon.

It had been a couples' weekend in a cabin. This was last year. The beginning of the divorce.

She knew that other men smelled differently from her husband's milkiness.

Maybe that was why she asked him to pull over at the road-side stand. Buy gourds, pumpkins to decorate their porch.

The lady with Keds and an apron with blue flowers, forget-me-nots, told her they had bittersweet vine, too.

[Wasn't it Sappho who wrote: "Eros once again limb-loosener whirls me sweetbitter"?
Sappho inverting the word to reveal passion's nature: first we taste the sweet.]

Just ten minutes earlier she had asked her husband, *I've never given you that look, have I? That crazy in-love look. Even when we were first dating?*

No, he said. *But we've always known that. It's okay.*

It was no longer okay.

She bought a Turkish turban, an Australian blue, two flattish Cinderellas, four butternuts. And the vine.

He asked for a third time: *Why do you want so much?*

□

All stories come from one of two:

A person loses something and tries to get it back (i.e. *Lolita*).

A person gets something and tries not to lose it (i.e. *Lolita*).

□

Prometheus from Zeus,
    Máui from Mudhens,
        Crow from Volcano,

Rabbit from Weasel,
    Grandmother
        Spider from Land

of Light and so on go
    the myths of taming fire.
        Stealing always at the core.

A loss. An offense. A way
    to incense the gods
        who knew to fear us,

who knew we would
    find a way
        to replace them.

☐

We, and no other animal, understand how to
start fire
               with flint, chert, pyrites,
pocket lint, feather down, pine moss, yucca
shreds, cedar bark, Bic.
                    How to stop it
with ash, water, flour, snuffer, hose, hook-n-
ladder,   stop-drop-and-roll.
                         How to hide it
in boiler tanks, engine blocks,   power grids.
                         How to wave
a finger through flame
          on Saturday night while drinking PBR.
                    This, even this,
makes us more
               advanced than the dog who
                                   sniffs
the same candle flame and whines.   Circles
three times,   then lies   back down.

□

Her father is a loss. Is the wood being cut down
and the cutter of that wood. Something decided
against and left behind. Something she left and is
better for leaving. There is a loss in this success
that she does not understand. Some days she can
almost name it: coldness. That's not it though. It is
more a fear of how easily she can leave a person. If
she cannot name the loss, doesn't that mean it was
all gain? A feeling closer to warmth?

She keeps returning to the base of this one large
maple that reminds her of a tree she sat under with
her father years ago. In her yard now, the maple
teems with poison ivy, one of the three leave-it-
be leaves as big as her palm. The vine haired and
never-ending. She has tried to kill it at least fifteen
times. Now she lets it grow, inspired by how it
cannot be controlled, cannot be touched. In the
black bag she carries with her to sit by this tree
is a bottle of water, some cooked white rice, and
something that she will not need: a knife.

◻

All stories tell us that in the beginning
was   darkness.   Dark-dark
and   silence.

            Maybe the first word
we finally said sitting around that fire,

everyone chewing on   red
colobus monkey, no one speaking was
                        Awkward.

We don't know
            that first word, that first word
that spiked a   whole   new   species,
but we can   speculate   it was:
                        Take.
As in: *I Give*   *this to you.*

                Both arms holding
out the meat, nodding toward the fire,
                        gesturing,

Sit,   sit down   with me.
The darkness quiets if we watch it together.

III.

For only the last 12,000 years in human history have we been alone on this planet without close relatives.

—Professor Diordia on the 2010 discovery of a new species, the Denisovans, who lived with modern man and interbred with Neanderthals.

SPACE BEARS AND DOXOLOGY

First reports described a run-away bear wearing
a space helmet. I'm not surprised. It is Tennessee,
and black bears gone alien are a possibility.

Here, life not as it seems is the hope. So, after
a month, wildlife rescuers tracked the scat to find
a juvenile male with his head stuck in a plastic

Walmart candy jar. Bulk-sized Jujyfruits. Honey
of all hives. The vet judged the bear one winter
away from death, having lost half its body weight.

He had learned to drink by lying down in shallow
streams where the water would seep in slow enough
to keep him from drowning. This story reminds me

how as a child I sewed pink curtains onto roach
motels, figuring they would like it better this way,
both coming and going. The curtains a lure

and an escort. I know the bear doesn't debate
about any of this, but if there were such a thing
as heaven, wouldn't it be the moment the jar

was removed, that rush of autumn air on his face?
No barrier between paw and tongue, touch
and taste. The world as it is now and ever shall be,

suddenly right before him, roughing cheeks
with sun on autumn mornings, and if he's lucky,
pricking his eyes with the sting of sleet come winter.

ESSAY ON COLLECTIVE PARANOIA

Metaphors, like epitaphs, must be fitting.
—Aristotle

I. The Incident: A New Method for Death and Metaphor[1]

Waiter carries a tray across the hotel
lobby to three men clustered in fat arm chairs.
Litvinenko[2] dunks in his tea bag. Brown-red
hovers then spreads like blood from a cut. L. sips,
nods *Yes, yes,* to men

he calls comrades. Someone has laced the water
or cup with Isotrope Polonium 210.
"The want of harmony between two things
is emphasized by their being placed side by side."
This is rhetoric,

according to Aristotle, and relates
to love, maybe marriage, and assassination.
Poison only effective if presented
harmoniously: old friends; damp, chilly day;
suggestion of tea.

---

1. From the Greek. Meta is a prefix signifying change, be that of place, order, condition, or nature. *Phor* is the verb for carrying. Metaphor literally means to carry change, from one object to another.
2. Alexander Litvinenko served in the Soviet KGB and publicly accused his superiors of assassinating Boris Berezovsky and bombing apartments to blame on terrorists. On November 1st, 2006, he walked into a London hospital and shortly died thereafter from radioactive polonium-210 poisoning, the first death of this kind. In this poem, he is referred to as "L."

Later, L. walks himself through the ER doors.
Doctors do not understand his sickness, so
the hospital charts resort to metaphor:
"His face is the color of the room's white wall;"
"Stomach a ping-pong ball

hit by a missile."[3] Metaphor is the mind
catching itself in a mistake, meaning we
learn the new through the known. We know hits, but not
like this hit. We know death but not like this death.
Metaphor—a bridge.

Tests come back clean. Still, L. insists: *They are*
killing me. Doctors think: *Metaphor; the pains*
and exams are difficult. Then, he is dead.
We loathe passive construction, demand subjects,
clear relationships.

So, next come questions: Whom did he meet? Unknown.
Tea? Darjeeling. Maybe they killed him when he said,
Please pardon me and left unaccompanied
his cup. L. had always feared walking
through crowded lobbies

under those recessed and shadowed ceilings. Air
cooler at his face than feet. Death and duty
merging in that air, the two terms indicating

---

3. Direct quotes from the doctor's charts as reported by James Geary in "The
First Assassination of the Twenty-first Century."

"what is fair or what is foul."[4] In the end,
his fears accurate.

II.   The Cause and Effect: Paranoia

Let us return to the lobby where L. sipped
his last tea, watched guests rush through revolving doors.
He suspected these moments of people coming
and going were significant. Lobby a place
to execute plans,

remake the self. Briefcases with proposals,
purses with passports, valises with garters.
Lobby carpet also loaded with design:
burgundy stars inside navy squares over
toast-yellow diamonds.

It is necessary, psychiatrists say,
to function by responding to fragments: "bits
of conversation, beginnings of actions…"[5]
We live on pieces. And attempt to piece all
into place. Someone

should be snapping photos while hiding behind
an indoor palm, eating a slice of folded
pizza. We know the wrongs we've done, the meanness
we've thought. Who knows what others might do? This is
not paranoia.

---

4. More of *Rhetoric* by Aristotle: "Both terms will indicate what is fair, or what is
foul, but not simply their fairness or foulness." Shakespeare later used this line.
5. Quote from Daniel Freeman and Phillipa A. Garety's *The Psychology of
Persecutory Delusions.*

P.[6] is akin to feeling loved. An attempt
at completeness,[7] an intimate friend. We tell P.
all fears. Who slighted us. How we deserved it.
And P. responds with: *Yes, worry! Yes, you're doomed;*
Then, we feel understood.

III.   Conclusion: Security Is All False

Concern for L. is not why we detail his death.
It's self-survival. P. can't protect if P.
can't imagine the threat.[8] The world churns and purrs
by forecasting our demise and devising
grand pre-emptive strikes.

All loss can be avoided: right liquid ounce,
right sexual mount, right hedge shape, right help mate,
right gruel, right bio-fuel, right SPF,
right laws against meth, right sugar substitute,
right Buddhist attitude,

and right polonium antidote will save us.
Reports assure that L.'s poisoning is not
possible for mass killings. But look here, P.
whispers, tapping a story on page D7,
U.S.A. Today.

---

6. "P." stands for paranoia.

7. The idea from Plato that we were once joined as one, then split into two. And love is a process of seeking that other to complete oneself. Trying to complete fragments, however, can also lead to wrong conclusions. Hence divorce, paranoia, and/or both.

8. A.k.a. the "clinical relevance of persecutory delusions" according to Freeman and Garety.

Men in hazmat suits carrying twelve-liter
oxygen tanks, radiation meters, screw
drills, deem a doorknob lethal, the door itself
a threat, and two hotel rooms unsafe for use.
They must remove bits

of the rooms, too: outlet plaques, curtain hooks,
the Gideon. Would have been covert except
for a snitch. Who took that picture of our charons
carrying a door through the lobby? A door walking
sideways through a door.

LITTLE VISIBLE SKY

Where I sit on my couch, I can't see the sky.
    Then a crow caws, and there it flies
across the mirror-silver glass of my coffee-table,
    angle just right to reflect a crosshatch

of window mullions, thick X of two power lines,
    and the underthrust—once, twice—
of that bird's wings rushing toward
    the blurry ring from yesterday's Coke can.

The oddity of a crow on a coffee-table—
    what's with me that isn't. Like the nurse today
knotting the blue plastic band around my arm,
    asking if I liked garlic minced or sliced on my pizza—

or not at all—she could understand that, too.
    Sliced, I said, although I was twenty years in the past
and staring at Father's arm, the moon-pale skin
    hooked in like an overloaded electrical outlet.

I worry about too many memories, less and less
    space to see what's in front of me—what's not.
"Little visible sky" is how one museum explained
    Renoir's paintings with their wine-flushed rich

sequestered beneath leafy trees, straw hats
    with fat blue ribbons, and that eye-patch of sky.
My painting is this: A table. A crow. A power line, wet
    and crossed, touching my wrist as I reach for a sip.

LEMONS ARE NOT NIPPLES

The tip of a lemon is not a nipple. The spine
of a book is not the spine of a man. No thing
is anything else. These are lies a poet tells to avoid
certain truths. The closest I have come to holding
a dying man's hand is witnessing a buffalo slaughtered.
Blood glugged out in rhythm with his tapering
heartbeat, but I couldn't tell when life switched off.

An hour maybe before the animal stilled. I think
of my father, a man never without a suitcase or place
to leave. It will happen while he waits to cross the street,
bag in hand. He doesn't notice the light changing, crowd
bumping his shoulders. Curb empties, yet he will remain,
drivers at the red light marveling at such stillness.
Less a man than a metaphor, pointing someplace else.

BEFORE THE CITY OPENS

Before the fast food signs dull their yellows
and reds for the day, before the cars cover

the pot-holed, buckled roads, the city belongs
to this man walking alone, wearing a suit,

a costume to cover his homelessness. Samsonite
in hand, he recites his daughter's phone number,

stringing the twos and fours like prayer beads.
He passes an iron sculpture of a man half-

sunk in the sidewalk, rowing a boat.
It slows time until almost yesterday.

Nearby, a woman brushes her teeth in a bank's
fountain. He waits to see if she spits. She does.

Yes, this sculpture is yesterday, the lead
man's knuckle big and hard as his head.

He checks the morning's obituaries.
Two men died older than he. Two younger.

There is never a next shore. Never a new.
Never a daughter who suddenly forgives.

WANTED: A PRETTY PICTURE

Sometimes, a discussion with the family is not possible.
Instead:
A woman takes a bike ride alone.
Sees the red bulge of carrion.
A maze of its own muscle on the back road.

A turkey buzzard,
So engorged it doesn't fly   when she bikes by.
Rather, it steadies its glare,   and she gives it space.

One could say this is the path
Too often taken: One that swerves clear.
One that prefers a certain type of calm:
Day-burned road-gravel,
Red-flicked and firm.

MY FATHER SEES THE SINGULARITY

A pigeon—
who forgets he's not starving—
clamps another pigeon's neck
down to the bone.
Gray body lifts off the ground—
an odd angle—sideways and stiff—a crooked tie.

Silence—not even a flap—
a clear indication
someone is winning.

What are the pigeons fighting over?
He kicks them out of the way—
reveals what looks like spilled French fries.
No. Not that. Squished intestines seep
from a third pigeon's carcass.

Boot-toe nudges the body
and off flops
a hind section swirling up
a whole new big bang of flies.

A singularity he's now broken apart.

If he were to retell the story—or our creation story:
Some lies. Some guess work. Some pride and repentance.
Mainly a sense of unstoppable
mistake

as if it were his body being created
or destroyed.
Lifted off the ground
by the neck.

word problems
home & school
they propose

stories obsess
why did the train
why did Ms. Australo

before sleep
now more plot lines
millions of foot-

how many footprints
how many names
for all the women

stories care little
we want
tell me a story

obsess over
fathers & daughters
x stands

over time
leave the station
want to see *over*

in beds
& hyper-links
prints glassed

do we mold
do we have
leaning over

about linear time
the mystery
someone

APE-LIKE

time by dotting
trains & stations
for something

by cross-hatching
five minutes late
instead of *into*

at bars
less who-dun-its
in labs to learn

from Lucy who knew
for Helen who left
the water's edge

about the distance
we want
somewhere says

two points
habilines & australopithecines
worth figuring

multiple motives
and nuclear?
the tall savannah grass?

same million-old lullaby
more why-I-dids
where the dead wanted to go

better fields weren't far?
her family to cross the Aegean?
searching for something more?

between A and B
the why the how the who
right now

EIGHT FAMILY SNAPSHOTS

i.
Orange chrysanthemums in the forest, metal-can light, photographer cooing, "Say Money!" and my father, brother, and I did. The sun was nowhere and would not have admitted to hanging out with us anyway.

I knew what the fake forest disguised, knew what the picture disguised, knew it was one more step toward being the adult who fists her hands, holds down the floor, and says, *No*.

The sun is busy today with homework, and so I sit, a grown woman, in my office, lights on at noon, feeling at once too thin and too full, slipping away and fattening up. I stand and it happens: the chrysanthemum blossoms from my elbow; a leaf moves from northwesterly wind.

ii.
My first act in this world was to wrap my hand around a crazy man's finger. This is why when I walk into a room people think, "Poised." Something charming about learning how to walk off-balance all one's life. *Thank you,* I should tell the crazy man. But I have this red canoe that's ready to shove out across the lake, my food sack of apples and peanut butter. There's no room for anyone else.

Right, I didn't make room.

My first act in this world was to wrap my hand around a crazy man's finger. This is why when I walk into a room, I turn around to see if I need to hold the door open for a wild-toed man in a black coat, rushing in before it closes.

iii.
That's Dad in the front row. Since his ego is so wide, it got the choice spot: elbows on the fake Olan Mills fence. We all cracked a different sport on our faces. Dad puffed like a cock-fight. I strived for underwater swimmer, face serene, absent. Lee would never admit it, but he hinted at ballerina. Before we came for our family photo, Lee and I discussed how drowning would be a wise way to take Dad down.

Once, Dad rose to a place made entirely of little top hats and gold-knobbed canes. And now, as adults? Simple, is what we pretend. And everything that means: milk, manners, red canoes, secrets, and strings of fat colored lights on the roof in December. The blink and the non-blink that don't wake the neighbors.

iv.
Stop it. Say it straight.

Fine, okay. It's noon. I'm standing in my office, and I still do not know what sort of person can ignore another person suffering. Can allow her own father to be homeless. Yet, I am that sort of person.

Another snapshot:

Once I snuck out of bed at hearing the *ah-ah-ah* of someone trying to breathe normally again. The *ahs* came from the kitchen, and I wanted to know what he was doing: drinking, smoking, watching porn? I hoped for something XXX. Excitement came when the slit of light from the fridge cut across his robed body. It closed black. And he sank down before even getting out a beer, sat cross-legged, sobbing.

Make it stop. Would you just make it stop? he asked no one in the room.

Even at age nine, I knew he was a man more lost than any child. Knew I wouldn't take him by the hand and lead him back to his room.

v.

During this same year, Dad told me how he had discovered a field of tiny bats that didn't hang in caves, but to grasses. Bats like grasshoppers. He'd rap one, and it wouldn't move. *You know what that's like,* he said. *You know.*

This was the year he could not sleep. This was the year his car hit a tree and then went into the field littered with the grasshopper bats. Nothing happened except the mirror broke off. Nothing happened except that I became the echo of that wreck. Something smooth, untouchable. Chiding.

vi.

The picture of now is too ordinary to mention: countertops with
the morning's toast crumbs. A plant wilting but not flopped-flat.
Everything in mid-action between living and lived. Shamelessly
overjoyed to feel the absence of him, I sometimes walk to the
linen closet and stare at the simplicity of stacked towels, red bag
of extra dog food. Fall is coming. I will plant butter lettuces and
kale for fun. My house manages to let in light from some window
throughout the day if there is light to be let in. The thing remains
inside that told me to crawl back to my bedroom and leave him
crying. It has teeth and a good pair of running shoes. Both the
dog chasing the runner and the runner fleeing from the dog.
When they meet at dusk once it finally cools enough to jog, they
first stiffen before realizing: *Oh, it's only you.*

vii.

I sense a confession is wanted. An office, like a ribcage, follows
orders that were decided before I came into the picture. I refuse
a confession because I have nothing and too much. So I've been
doodling faces, taking naps, avoiding. I fiddle with facts. The
width between eyes determines the size of the brain. It's simply an
issue of space and giving space. Like man's determination to find
miniature bats hanging in grass after a car wreck.

xiii.

The red canoe that shoves out over the Saran-wrapped waters—
this is my selfishness. I would not trade it. In that contest for
survival, where does selfishness fit in? I have a dog that I love

partly because she'll stop eating when I near her bowl in case I want her food. Then again, subservience is what keeps a beta alive. Maybe the dog that bites off half a child's lip is giving in a way I don't understand. I can cross the lake to the other shore and make a fire with twigs and trash, make a campsite, say: *I built it. I'll sleep here. I'll leave it. And I'll do it all again.* My own hand connects the dots for me, points out each dipper, each snake, each indisposed queen.

BARDO (2)

Yeah, I'm having to watch that right now,
my brother said, "That," being the slow death of our dad,
Spike.

My brother was at the pool talking to a woman
with a prison tat, her boobs somehow
up and full as two oranges.
Bikini tops are amazing things, he thought,
not fully understanding the simplicity of synthetics.

        What she said next, the woman sunbathing
        with the tits and prison tat,
was that traditional Japanese Buddhists believe
no one is fully alive until the 7th birthday.
    Life something you become filled with—
    like water pouring from a pitcher into the body.

Dying takes a long time, too, he said, thinking about
Spike pissing himself by the packaged Swiss
and shredded Mozzarella in the Kroger aisle.
That darkness spreading across the crotch of his tan pants
        and moving down his right leg in a wobbly line
        like water pouring from a pitcher.
The look in his eyes: scared, apologetic.
And then he blinked. Smiled.
        Began humming "In the Room—"
        a song he'd danced to with all the girls in the fifties.
He was no longer there, no longer in Kroger,

when he stepped forward and reached out both arms
toward the brightly lit rows of cheese,
all the while humming, *Let's keep on dancing,*
keep on dancing,
when we're alone in the room.

THALIA CHASING GRAPEFRUIT

—After Robert Hass

The grapefruit rolls downhill,
that motion June morning.
        Fruit heavy with seven days
        rain, climbing ants,
        plump, white-veined seeds.
The wide paws of the golden spaniel
flail after it like a conductor criss-crossing his arms
in a final dare of energy.

Evolution, somewhere then and now,
went a little manic, did a step-ball-change tap movement
        and then the fish walked,
the seed split,
wet, craving more.

But we should take away agency.
        The seed sprouted.
        The sprout seeded.

There are limits to knowledge, limits to
describing the comedic effect of Thalia finally squashing
her teeth into the fruit, flipping
her head high and prancing by,
drooling juice.

        Sometimes it's best when a poem fails.
Reminds us of what we can't obtain. Like simplicity.
Like dog. Sunlight.
Rolling grapefruit.

ARGUMENT (2)

Wind bending a grove
Of bamboo. Thin-trunked.
Sound of an opening door.
So, I thought of my father.

Of our loblollies, our axes, our
History and our longer history
Detailed in tooth size, pelvis
Flares, hyoid bones, guts—

But why? my father interrupted.

I answered: *Remember the globe I had as a kid? The one that sat crooked on the desk, unable to turn. The bulb inside burned out, unable to light the broken blue oceans. I've walked on dots I once pointed to. Looked down the 200-foot shaft where archeologists are finding a new branch of human beings. Smelled freshly uncovered 10,000-year-old dirt; it smells like our dirt: ripe with ash and clay, sunning bone and lost rain.*

Don't, he said, pointing at me, his finger shining with sugar. *I've told you a hundred times: don't you ever bury me in this ground.*

And I've told you: This is the only story we know, the story we keep telling. How it all falls. How it all ends. A slow descent. A piling of dirt over face.

NOTES

Epigraphs by Charles Darwin are from the first edition of *On the Origin of Species.*

"Pig and a Bottle" is set in Sulawesi, Indonesia where death is not only revered, but focused on throughout life. Therefore, the funeral is a grand event attended by many, including strangers. Buffalo and pigs are sacrificed to escort the dead to heaven and to provide the community nourishment.

Two poems in this collection are titled after the concept of "bardo," which is a Tibetan word to signify intermediate states of existence like the time before birth or after death. The term can also be used metaphorically to signal a time when our usual existence is suspended such as during periods of severe illness.

"Normalization of Deviance" derives its title from accident investigation boards for both Challenger and Columbia. They asked why NASA allowed O-rings and foam insulation to continue being used despite past problems. Since errors with the O-rings and the foam insulation had become typical, engineers and managers testified how they began to see these flaws as part of the process. Diane Vaughan, who wrote *The Challenger Launch Decision* (University of Chicago Press, 1996), gave this type of rationalizing behavior a name: the "Normalization of Deviance."

"Memory Corruption: Cinderella Always Knew She'd Lose a Shoe" takes as its subject the human tendency to inaccurately remember events. While many people consider this a negative trait, recent evolutionary research suggests that it has aided our survival by allowing us to respond with insight to similar, future situations. Those with paranoia have far more memory corruption than others without the disease.

The title of the poem, "It Would Be Nice to Have a Whole Complete Male," refers to the fossilized skeleton known as The Hobbit, which is the most recent, confirmed discovery of a distinct species named Homo floresiensis. The skeleton was found on a remote island, Flores, in Indonesia. This skeleton suggests that humans may be more subject to evolutionary forces than we think; that other species might also have existed; and that perhaps Asia had its own rate of evolutionary changes. What is known is that this species lived 12,000 years ago, at the same time as modern man, but displays features that existed two to three millions years earlier such as large guts, small brains, and wrists typical to that of Australopithecines.

"The Branches, the Axe, the Missing" is informed by research found in Robert Wrangham's book *Catching Fire: How Cooking Made Us Human* (Perseus Books, 2009).

"Upright but Ape-Like" is a descriptor of Australopithecines, who were not much more intelligent than apes, but who were bipedal. "Lucy" is the most famous of these found fossils. Part of her significance stems from the fact that scientists once believed intelligence increased and then we became bipedal. Lucy's hips dispute that. The question remains as to why humans ever gave up the benefits of being able to climb for being able to walk on two feet.

ACKNOWLEDGMENTS

The author gratefully acknowledges the publications in which the following poems, sometimes in different versions, first appeared:

Alaska Quarterly Review: "Lemons Are Not Nipples," "Space Bears and Doxology," and "Wanted: A Pretty Picture"

Cutthroat: Sections II, XV-XVI of *The Branches, the Axe, the Missing*

Denver Quarterly: "Argument (1)," "Memory Corruption: Cinderella Always Knew She'd Lose a Shoe," and "Thalia Chasing Grapefruit"

Diagram: "Life is Long and Full of Action and Color"

The Freeman: "The Black River" titled in this collection as "Before the City Opens"

Kenyon Review Online: "Essay on Collective Paranoia"

Luna Luna: "Pig and a Bottle"

New South: "It Would Be Nice to Have a Whole Complete Male"

Ninth Letter: "Bardo (1)"

North American Review: "Architecture of the Veil" and "Bardo (2)"

Offending Adam: Sections III, IV, VI, and XIII of *The Branches, the Axe, the Missing*

Passages North: "Upright but Ape-Like"

Poems and Plays: "The Diagnosis: Paranoid Schizophrenia" and "My Father Speaks of Thieves"

Prairie Schooner: "Eight Family Snapshots" and "My Father's Nipples"

Radar: "Signs and Symptoms [May] Include Delusions"

Swink: "Divining"

Tar River Poetry Review: "Little Visible Sky"

The Southern Poetry Anthology, Volume VI: Tennessee reprinted "Divining."

The Branches, the Axe, the Missing, winner of the Black River chapbook competition, was previously published by Black Lawrence Press/Dzanc Books.

GRATITUDE

To the editorial team at Black Lawrence Press, especially Diane Goettel, Angela Leroux-Lindsey, and Kit Frick, thank you. I could not have asked for a more energetic, dedicated group of women who share my love for poetry, science, and the pleasure of reading a beautiful book.

I would also like to thank the graduate program in English at the University of Tennessee and especially my committee who read (and reread) my dissertation, which became this collection. To the chair Marilyn Kallet, a force of poetic power, to Arthur Smith with his light hand who always had a book to recommend and to Amy Billone, a scholar of silence, who encouraged me to say what *I* had silenced—I am forever in your debt. And to my fellow cohorts at UT—Christian Gerard, Jesse Graves, Tawnysha Greene, Otis Haschemeyer, Chase Irwin, Darren Jackson, Kierstyn Lamour, George Pate, Joshua Robbins, Tim Sisk, and Bradford Tice—your work inspired my own.

While at Emerson College, I had the good fortune to work with Bill Knott, Gail Mazur, David Daniel, and John Skoyles. Each of these poets has left an indelible mark, for which I am grateful. And my dear friend at Emerson, Shira Shaiman, who recently passed away, taught me to love poetry for its power to preserve us—a lesson I'm only now fully understanding.

To my colleagues at Eastern Illinois University, where I have recently found a home, I'd like to say how supported I have felt and to especially express my gratitude to our department chair, Dana Ringuette, who understands the demanding yet gratifying profession of being both a professor and an active writer. To my fellow creative writing colleagues Olga Abella, Lania Knight, Daiva Markelis, Robin Murray, Ruben Quesada, and to my writer's group in town Roxane Gay, Ruth Hoberman, Mary Maddox, Lee Roll, and Angela Vietto—thank you for all of your kindness and wisdom.

To my family who supported me when they weren't even sure what they were supporting. My mother Rita Tate, my stepfather Robert Tate, my aunt Anita, and my brother have all shown such love and understanding.

Finally, this book would not have come into being without the support and editorial insights of my husband, Adam Prince. I am continually astounded by the love that surrounds.

Photo: John Black

Charlotte Pence's poetry merges the personal with the scientific by engaging with current evolutionary theory. A professor of English and creative writing at Eastern Illinois University, Pence is the author of two award-winning poetry chapbooks and editor of *The Poetics of American Song Lyrics* (University Press of Mississippi, 2012). She received her M.F.A. from Emerson College and Ph.D. from University of Tennessee. Her poetry has appeared or is forthcoming in *Denver Quarterly, Kenyon Review Online, North American Review, Prairie Schooner, Rattle, The Southern Review* and many other journals. This is her first full-length collection.